THE JEWISH QUARTERLY

The Jewish Quarterly is published four times a year
by The Jewish Quarterly Pty Ltd

Publisher: Morry Schwartz

ISBN 9781760645458 E-ISBN 9781743824177
ISSN 0449010X E-ISSN 23262516

Subscriptions 1 year print & digital (4 issues): $109.99 AUD | £55 GBP |
$75 USD. 1 year digital only: $64.99 AUD | £35 GBP | $45 USD. Payment may
be made by Mastercard or Visa. Payment includes postage and handling.

Subscribe online at jewishquarterly.com or email subscribe@jewishquarterly.com
Correspondence should be addressed to: The Editor, The Jewish Quarterly,
22–24 Northumberland Street, Collingwood VIC 3066 Australia
Phone +61 3 9486 0288 Email enquiries@jewishquarterly.com

The Jewish Quarterly is published under licence from the
Jewish Literary Trust Limited, which exercises a governance function.

UK Company Number: 01189861. UK Charity Commission Number: 268589.

Founding Editor: Jacob Sonntag.

Editor: Jonathan Pearlman. Associate Editor: Jo Rosenberg.
Additional Editing: Emma Bowers. Publishing Manager: Lilith Elenberg.
Publishing Coordinator: Noa Abrahams. Management: Elisabeth Young.
Design: John Warwicker and Tristan Main. Production: Marilyn de Castro.
Typesetting: Tristan Main.

Issue 260, May 2025

THE JEWISH QUARTERLY

The Z Word

Reclaiming Zionism

Adam Kirsch is a poet and critic whose books include *On Settler Colonialism: Ideology, Violence and Justice* and *The Revolt Against Humanity: Imagining a Future Without Us*. He lives in New York City.

The Jewish Quarterly is grateful for support from:

The Anglo–Jewish Association

The Exilarch's Foundation

The Polonsky Foundaton

The Z Word

Reclaiming Zionism

Adam Kirsch

1.

In June 2024, Israeli special forces rescued four hostages from the Nuseirat refugee camp in the Gaza Strip. The hostages, kidnapped in the Hamas attack on October 7, 2023, were being held in residential apartment buildings by civilian supporters of Hamas, and when the Israeli raid met with heavy resistance, many Palestinians were killed – almost 300, according to the Gaza health ministry, which doesn't distinguish between combatants and civilians; less than 100, according to the Israel Defense Forces (IDF).

Two days later, pro-Palestinian student groups at several New York City colleges responded by declaring a "citywide day of rage". The main protest took place on Wall Street outside the Nova Music Festival Exhibition, a travelling commemoration of the 370 young people killed by Hamas at a music festival in southern Israel.

Demonstrators chanted, "Long live the intifada" and "Israel go to hell", while setting off flares and waving Palestinian flags.

That evening, a subway passenger took a twenty-second video showing a packed carriage in which about a dozen college-age protesters are crowded in with other passengers. While the train stands in a station with the doors open, a bearded young man wearing reflective sunglasses and a keffiyeh around his neck calls out, "Raise your hand if you're a Zionist! This is your chance to get out!" The other protesters repeat the words in a chant, using the "mic check" technique common at demonstrations. When there is no response, he declares, "Okay, no Zionists, we're good!" and a woman echoes, "We don't want no Zionists here."

The man was clearly still feeling the festive atmosphere of the day of rage: at the end of the clip, he chuckles and lets out a celebratory "Woo!" But when the video began to circulate on social media, and then made the local news, New Yorkers were less amused. Mayor Eric Adams described the incident as "reprehensible and vile" and the NYPD issued a wanted poster for the bearded man. By the end of the month, the 24-year-old New York City native, a lab technician, turned himself in to face a misdemeanour charge of "coercion".

For many American Jews, the subway video was like the scene at the end of a horror movie where the survivors are finally breathing easy, and then suddenly the monster's hand sticks up out of the grave. It was the kind of episode that used to be common in Jewish life, but that we never expected to see in twenty-first-century New York: bullies using threats and contempt to drive Jews out of a public space, daring them to fight back, laughing when they don't. *Juden raus*, the Germans used to say – "Jews get out." Does it make a difference to say "Zionists get out" instead?

That question now stands at the centre of Jewish life around the world. In his Booker Prize–winning novel, *The Finkler Question*, British novelist Howard Jacobson wrote that the word Jew "was a password to madness. Jew. One little word with no hiding place for reason in it. Say 'Jew' and it was like throwing a bomb." That was in 2010; now the word "Zionist" has largely taken its place. Indeed, calling someone a Zionist isn't just like throwing a bomb; for those who use it as an insult, it justifies – and sometimes accompanies – throwing actual bombs.

> Juden raus, *the Germans used to say – "Jews get out." Does it make a difference to say "Zionists get out" instead?*

The New York subway incident was widely publicised because it was caught on video, but in the long list of confrontations and provocations Jews have experienced since October 2023, it is far from the worst. The Anti-Defamation League has been keeping a tally of anti-Zionist attacks around the world. In November 2023, just weeks after the Hamas raid, a school in Germany was vandalised with the slogan "Kill all Zionists!", and stickers reading, "Hamas, Hamas, Zionists to the Gas" appeared on walls in the Netherlands. In December, a man wielding a knife entered a Jewish day-care centre in France and told the director, "You're a Jew. You're a Zionist. Five of us are going to rape you and cut you up like they did in Gaza." In February 2024, the owner of a souvenir shop in Brazil was accosted by atourist who called her a "Zionist baby killer". In March, a student was barred from entering a classroom at Sciences Po, a university in Paris, by a group of about sixty people chanting, "Don't let her in. She's a Zionist." In April, an Orthodox man in Milan was shoved to the ground after being told, "Fucking Zionist! You kill children!"

In the United States, the most conspicuous aggression against Zionists has taken place at universities. In April 2024, pro-Palestinian students at the University of California, Los Angeles, set up an encampment in the centre of campus. When students they identified as Jewish approached, the protesters formed a human chain to block their access to libraries and classrooms, while chanting, "Zionist! Zionist!" In January 2024, a student at Columbia University said during an Instagram livestream, "Zionists don't deserve to live" and "Be grateful that I'm not just going out and murdering Zionists." He was suspended and is now suing the university for violating his rights.

Anti-Zionists, at least the shrewder among them, recognise that the post-Holocaust taboo against antisemitism has not entirely disappeared from Western society, and they make a point of insisting that hostility to Zionists is not the same as hostility to Jews. Zionism, after all, is not an inherited religious or ethnic identity; it is a political belief, which everyone is free to accept or reject. And some Jews do reject it. According to an October 2024 poll by the Manhattan Institute, 5 per cent of American Jewish voters say they are not supporters of the Jewish state.

That 5 per cent is well represented on elite university campuses, and when pro-Palestine encampments sprang up in April 2024, many pointed to the participation of Jewish students as proof that they could not be antisemitic. At Columbia, the Gaza Solidarity encampment even hosted a Seder, organised by the campus chapter of Jewish Voice for Peace. "As the largest anti-Zionist Jewish organization in the world," JVP's website declares, "we unequivocally reject the conflation of antisemitism with anti-Zionism and reaffirm in the strongest terms that there is no place for antisemitism in our movements."

They must be confounded, then, to find that so much anti-Zionist rhetoric employs the traditional grammar of Jew-hatred. Calling for Zionists to be sent to gas chambers invokes the Holocaust. Saying that Zionists love to kill babies echoes the old Christian blood libel. No wonder so many members of "our movements" do not recognise any distinction between attacking Zionists and attacking Jews. After all, they know that Zionism has to do with the Jewish state, and the Jewish state has to do with Jews, so it follows that any Jewish person or institution is an appropriate target for anti-Zionist agitation.

Thus, in March 2024, masked men entered two kosher delis in the United Kingdom and demanded to know whether staff and customers supported the IDF. In June, students at Baruch College, part of New York City's public university system, staged a protest in front of the school's chapter of Hillel, a nationwide Jewish student organisation, using the slogan "Hillel Stands with Genocide". According to the *Jewish Telegraphic Agency* account, one protester "brandished a banner that had a swastika inside a Star of David while shouting, 'Synagogue of Satan'" – a phrase from the New Testament that has been used to malign Jews for 2000 years.

Other anti-Zionist activists are furthering the cause by compiling public lists of Jewish individuals and institutions, including their addresses. In Massachusetts, a group called the Mapping Project created a website showing the locations of 497 "local entities and networks" they accuse of offering "institutional support for the colonization of Palestine". These include the Jewish Teen Foundation of Greater Boston, the Hillel Council of New England and Harpoon Brewery, a craft beer company that did business with an Israeli water-purification company. The stated purpose of the map, which can be found at mapliberation.org, is to "dismantle" the targeted organisations: "Every entity has an address, every network can be disrupted."

Other online activists have compiled lists of Zionists in specific professional fields in order to encourage boycotts. A Facebook group called Chicago Anti-Racist Therapists shared "a list of therapists/practices with Zionist affiliations that we should avoid referring clients to". The only thing the twenty-six therapists on the list had in common was a Jewish-sounding last name. "I do not post publicly about the conflict or about Israel at all, ever," one of them told *Jewish Insider*.

A similar list titled, "Is your fav author a zionist???" went viral in May 2024. Anyone could edit the Google Doc and add writers' names, colour-coding them to indicate their political stance: red for "pro-Israel/Zionist", blue for "pro-Palestinian/anti-Zionist" and other shades for borderline cases. "If YES, it's suggested you do not give them any money (purchasing their books, streaming their shows/movies) or promote their work on any social platforms," the document stated. As with the list of therapists, many writers were included simply on the basis of having a Jewish name, whether or not they had ever publicly voiced an opinion about Israel or Zionism.

It is tempting to dismiss the "fav authors" list as one of the countless bits of flotsam that surface in our social media feeds and then disappear. But the attitude it expresses has real-world consequences. One of the names on the list was Salman Rushdie, who had a mixed rating: he had taken part in an event called Books for Gaza, but also participated in a festival organised by PEN America, described as "an org that supports the genocide". PEN, a nonprofit

Whenever people are doxxed for being Zionists, that is the menacing subtext: we know where you live

writers' group that advocates for the "freedom to write", had to cancel its annual festival and literary awards in 2024 after many writers withdrew in protest of the organisation's failure to publicly describe the Israeli invasion of Gaza as a genocide. The criticism focused on PEN's chief executive, Suzanne Nossel, who was blamed in one open letter for her "longstanding commitments to Zionism" and for "Zionist propaganda". Nossel, who is Jewish, resigned from PEN six months later.

Meanwhile, in Australia, a WhatsApp group chat of some 600 Jewish academics and creative professionals had its messages leaked online in February 2024. The group was started after October 7 by Jews who felt professionally ostracised by anti-Israel peers – a feeling amply justified by the treatment they received as part of the "Zio600", as they were called online, using a term that originated on the antisemitic far right. One high school teacher on the list said that her employer received phone calls accusing her of being complicit in genocide. A Jewish family in Melbourne went into hiding after being sent a photograph of their child with the message, "I know where you live."

Whenever people are doxxed for being Zionists, that is the menacing subtext: we know where you live, we can hurt you any time we want to. In June 2024, the home of the director of the Brooklyn Museum was targeted by vandals who left a banner reading, "Anne Pasternak/Brooklyn Museum/White Supremacist Zionist." They also painted the door and windows with red triangles, a symbol used by Hamas to designate Israeli military targets, which has become popular with anti-Israel protesters.

Why blame the war in Gaza on the Brooklyn Museum – an estimable local institution that lives in the shadow of Manhattan mega-museums such as the Metropolitan and the Museum of Modern Art? Even those who targeted it had no real explanation. Two weeks before Pasternak's home was attacked, about thirty demonstrators occupied the Brooklyn Museum's lobby, in what *ARTnews* politely called "one of the most fervent Gaza solidarity actions yet to descend on a New York City art institution". The group responsible, calling itself Cultural Front for Free Palestine, stated that it wanted "the disclosure of funds from donors and trustees who are heavily implicated in the Occupation", but didn't name any. Earlier protests had blamed the museum for accepting donations from Bank of New York Mellon, because it invests in an index fund that includes the stock of an Israeli defence company.

Such connections to Israel are so tenuous that the protesters' focus on the Brooklyn Museum can only be explained by convenience. Certain parts of Brooklyn are home to a lot of young people whose identities are founded on an interest in the arts and radical politics. (One of the people arrested for vandalising Pasternak's home was a 28-year-old freelance illustrator.) For them, if for no one else, the Brooklyn Museum represents authority – but a lenient one, which is unlikely to call the police on people who invade the lobby to beat drums and blow whistles, or climb the roof to hang a banner reading, "Free Palestine/Divest from Genocide".

But targeting the director's home – along with those of three other members of the museum's board – represented a significant escalation. The threat was implicit but unmistakable, and this time three people were arrested on charges that included "criminal mischief as a hate crime". As the Brooklyn district attorney explained: "These defendants allegedly targeted museum board members with threats and antisemitic graffiti based on their perceived heritage."

As is often the case, however, the connection between anti-Zionism and antisemitism wasn't crystal clear. Some of the trustees targeted had "Jewish-sounding last names", as the prosecutor stated, but others didn't; and in fact, the same was true of the three defendants. If a Jewish activist paints the word "Zionist" on the front door of a non-Jew, can it really be described as an act of antisemitism? What about when a Jewish professor shares a social media post demanding, "Don't normalize Zionism. Don't normalize Zionists taking up space," as Maura Finkelstein, an anthropologist at Muhlenberg College, did after the October 7 attack?

In dealing with the current blizzard of attacks on Zionism, Jewish communities have often resorted to the same technique as the Brooklyn district attorney – treating anti-Zionism as another name for antisemitism. The US House of Representatives endorsed this idea in a December 2023 resolution that "clearly and firmly states that anti-Zionism is anti-Semitism". The symbolic resolution passed with 311 votes in favour and only fourteen against, including prominent left-wing Democrats Alexandria Ocasio-Cortez, Ilhan Omar and Rashida Tlaib. (There were also ninety-two abstentions, mainly Democrats who objected to the resolution as a toothless partisan exercise.)

Equating anti-Zionism with antisemitism also makes emotional sense, since most Jews feel that some kind of attachment to Israel is a central part of their Jewish identity. A 2021 Pew Research survey found that "eight in ten US Jews say caring about Israel is an essential or important part of what being Jewish means to them". Polls in the UK and Australia have similar results. This does not mean that these Jews are uncritically supportive of everything Israel's government and military do. But they are not willing to renounce the Jewish state any more than they would renounce Judaism itself. Indeed, the majority of non-Orthodox Jews would probably sooner deny the traditional tenets of Jewish faith – divine authorship of the Torah, for instance – than declare that Zionism is evil and Israel should not exist. But as the crisis that began on October 7, 2023 passes the eighteen-month mark, it is becoming clear that fighting anti-Zionism as if it were antisemitism is not an effective long-term strategy. For if Zionism comes to be widely seen as morally impermissible – if, as many young people in particular are coming to believe, it is synonymous with racism, colonialism and genocide – then the fraying taboo against antisemitism will not be strong enough to protect it. Rather, as we have already begun to see, the toxicity of Zionism will erode that taboo.

At this moment, when the legitimacy of Zionism is under threat, we should remember a principle laid down long ago by the political philosopher Hannah Arendt. Arendt's own lifelong relationship with Zionism and

When people are attacked for being Zionist, they cannot respond by demanding protection as Jews

Israel was complicated. But in 1941, when she settled in New York City after escaping German-occupied France, she believed that the most urgent priority for Jews was the creation of a Jewish army in Palestine.

In an article for a German-language émigré newspaper, Arendt argued that it was not enough for Jews in the Yishuv, the pre-state Jewish settlement in the Land of Israel, to enlist individually in the army of Britain, which at the time ruled Palestine under a mandate from the League of Nations. Rather, Jews in Palestine and beyond must "join the battle against Hitler as Jews, in Jewish battle formations under a Jewish flag". She had no illusions that a Jewish army, which would necessarily be small, could turn the tide in World War II. Rather, Arendt wrote, Jews needed to learn an important political truth: "You can only defend yourself as the person you are attacked as. A person attacked as a Jew cannot defend himself as an Englishman or a Frenchman. The world would only conclude that he is simply not defending himself."

In the same way, when people or institutions are attacked today for being Zionist, they cannot respond by demanding protection as Jews. If the only defence against anti-Zionism is to claim that it is really antisemitism, the world will conclude that Zionism cannot be defended. And if Jews embrace an indefensible ideology, it is rational to regard them as a force for evil. Zionists become people it is virtuous to hate.

2.

This, of course, is a familiar role for Jews in Western civilisation. What infuriated generations of European Christians about Jews wasn't simply that they weren't Christians, but that the truth of Christianity should have been obvious to them – it was all around them, every right-thinking person agreed on it. Yet they continued to reject it. What could explain this stubbornness except superlative wickedness?

In his notorious 1543 tract *On the Jews and Their Lies*, Martin Luther expatiated on this Jewish quality:

When you lay eyes on or think of a Jew you must say to your-self: Alas, that mouth which I there behold has cursed and execrated and maligned every Saturday my dear Lord Jesus Christ, who has redeemed me with his precious blood; in addition, it prayed and pleaded before God that I, my wife and children, and all Christians might be stabbed to death and perish miserably.

In the twenty-first century West, it can be hard to understand this kind of hatred. A religious inquisitor burning a Jew or a heretic at the stake seems to us simply an inexplicable relic of barbarism, like gladiator fights or bear-baiting. But Luther's tone of nearly insane rage is precisely the way Zionism is now commonly discussed on social media. Search for the word "Zionist" on X, and you will find hundreds of thousands of posts like these, selected at random over the space of a few days:

Zionism is a cancer. Zionists are Satanists.

They make me sick. They're so EVIL.

Zionists are literally the most evil people to walk this earth.

Look at their eyes. Zionism turns you into a demon.

No wonder Meta, the parent company of Facebook and Instagram, announced in 2024 that it would begin flagging the word "Zionist" as potential hate speech, and "remove content that targets 'Zionists' with dehumanising comparisons, calls for harm, or denials of existence". People don't luxuriate in hatred in this way if they feel secretly ashamed of it, as most educated people do when they express racist or sexist views. This is the language of proud, fully justified hatred. Perhaps the only other group it is common to hear attacked in this way is child molesters.

In the imagination of Christian Europe, murdering children was the archetypal Jewish crime, because it is the most evil act human beings can imagine. Not only did it make sense that an evil people would commit such an act, but the belief that they were committing it, or that it was only a matter of time before they did, also justified punitive violence. "Evil shall have what evil will deserve," says the magistrate in Chaucer's *The Prioress's Tale*, as he orders the Jews of his town to be torn to pieces by horses for the crime of cutting the throat of a Christian child.

There is thus a kind of atavistic inevitability about the way Israel's war in Gaza has been transformed, in anti-Zionist discourse, into a conspiracy to murder children. Of course, while Jews never killed Christian children to use their blood for baking matzah, Jewish soldiers in Gaza have killed Arab children. The exact figures are disputed, but according to the Gaza health ministry, which is part of the Hamas government, by March 2025 Israel's invasion had killed 50,000 people, of whom about 15,000 were under the age of eighteen. Israel claims that about 20,000 of the dead were fighters, which would mean the ratio of civilian to military deaths was low compared to past military conflicts in dense urban areas.

What is beyond dispute is that the war has killed and injured many thousands of innocent people. In December 2024, the *New York Times* reported that after the October 7 attack, the Israeli military dramatically loosened its rules of engagement in Gaza. In the past, airstrikes that would endanger civilians had to be approved by a senior commander. Now even mid-level officers were given "the authority to risk killing up to 20 civilians" in a strike. This kind of warfare has turned global public opinion against Israel to an unprecedented degree.

In the face of so much Palestinian suffering, it may feel irrelevant to criticise the terms in which people express their outrage. But there is no way to understand today's anti-Zionism without analysing how the war in Gaza is interpreted by drawing on old patterns of thinking about Jews and Judaism. Only this can explain why Israel's war, uniquely among military conflicts, is regularly described as a "war on children", including by UNICEF.

This phrase has never been applied to the American invasion of Iraq and subsequent civil war, which according to a study published in 2013 caused half a million deaths, or to the Russian invasion of Ukraine, where the civilian death toll is at least 40,000. But for many people, especially in the Arab world, it is an article of faith that the purpose of Israel's invasion of Gaza is not to destroy Hamas and prevent future October 7–style attacks, but to kill Palestinian children. As the Palestinian Information Center, a news website, explained in September 2024, in terms Luther would have appreciated:

> Ears that delight in the screams of children, eyes that delight in seeing the remains of infants, pictures of soldiers taken next to the bodies of victims who have seen little of life, politicians and media professionals who boast of their ecstasy when the number of young dead increases. All these models have only come together in Israel that is waging a mad war on all manifestations of innocence in the Gaza Strip, and at its heart are women and children.

Similarly, it is an article of faith among Western progressives that Israel is committing genocide in Gaza. This claim is hard to understand if the word is being used in its dictionary sense, as "the deliberate and systematic destruction of a racial, political, or cultural group". In the Holocaust, 6 million Jews were killed and Eastern European Jewish civilisation ceased to exist. In the Armenian genocide of 1915–16, the Turks killed up to 1 million Armenians, effectively erasing that people from the Ottoman Empire. In the Rwandan genocide of 1994, Hutu mobs killed more than 800,000 mostly Tutsi victims in just 100 days, more than two-thirds of the country's total Tutsi population.

The war in Gaza bears no resemblance to those events, neither in scale nor intent. If Israel's goal was to destroy the Palestinian people, it would be hard to explain why, for instance, the Israeli military paused operations twice, in September and October 2024, so a UN campaign could administer polio vaccines to 600,000 Palestinian children. As terrible as the death toll in Gaza is, more than ten times as many people have been killed in the Syrian civil war since 2011. Almost 100 times as many were killed in the Congo War of 1998–2003, which few people in the West have even heard of. Yet those conflicts are never described as genocides. Why is the term so insistently applied to the war in Gaza?

One reason is that the image of Israel as a genocidal country was well established in many parts of academia, the left and the Arab world long before October 7. During the 2014 Israel–Hamas war, in which about 2000 Palestinians were killed, Mahmoud Abbas, head of the Palestinian Authority, told the UN General Assembly that Israel was waging "a war of genocide". During the 2009 Israel–Hamas war, in which 1400 Palestinians were killed, Venezuela's president, Hugo Chávez, said that, "The Israelis were looking for an excuse to exterminate the Palestinians," and demanded, "What was it if not genocide?"

Before any of these wars were fought, Patrick Wolfe, the influential Australian scholar who helped to create the flourishing academic field of settler colonial studies, warned in a landmark 2006 paper, "Settler Colonialism and the Elimination of the Native", that "as Palestinians become more and more dispensable, Gaza and the West Bank become less and less like Bantustans and more and more like reservations (or, for that matter, like the Warsaw Ghetto)". The implication was

> *To recast Israeli Jews as the agents of genocide is to reverse the rationale for the country's existence*

that Israel was preparing to exterminate the Palestinians in the same way that the Nazis exterminated the Jews concentrated in the Warsaw Ghetto.

In 2006, the population of Gaza was about 1.3 million; today it is 2.1 million. This statistic alone makes clear that charges of genocide and extermination against Israel were never intended to be statements of fact. Rather, they express a sense that the existence of Israel as a Jewish state itself constitutes a kind of genocide, because it is inimical to the national interest of Palestinian Arabs. Sometimes this idea is stated explicitly, as when pro-Hamas marchers in Cuba chanted, "Free, free Palestine/Israel is genocide."

More common is the kind of implicit association made by US congresswoman Rashida Tlaib in May 2024, when she proposed a resolution stating: "The Nakba did not end in 1948, but continues to this day as Israeli forces commit genocide in Gaza." The Nakba, or "catastrophe", is what Palestinians call the flight or expulsion of some 750,000 Arabs during Israel's war of independence. Tlaib proposed her resolution to mark Nakba Day, which Palestinians observe at the same time as Israel's Independence Day. (The resolution did not advance to a vote in Congress.)

In associating the Nakba with genocide, the resolution echoes a large body of academic discourse. For example, Damien Short of the University of London writes in his book *Redefining Genocide* that the Nakba should be included in "a broader sociological understanding of genocide", which defines it not as mass killing but as any historical event in which "individuals are unable to connect to the culture and social ethos of their community". And since this kind of genocide "can be understood as a process", Short concludes, "then it is ongoing and not limited to the events in 1948".

Similarly, Marouf Hasian Jr of the University of Utah argues in his book *Debates on Colonial Genocide in the 21st Century* that "the proto-typical, Auschwitz-centered way" of defining genocide as "intentional large-scale mass murder" must be overturned. Hasian argues that we must "treat genocidal recognition as a rhetorical achievement": in other words, when enough people decide to call something a genocide, it becomes one.

We can see this happening before our eyes with the war in Gaza, but the effort to redescribe the events of 1948 as a genocide of Palestinians is long-standing. The political motivation is not hard to understand. In the Western world, the Holocaust is the archetypal genocide – the word itself was invented by Raphael Lemkin, a Jewish refugee from Poland, during World War II – and the Jews are the archetypal victims of genocide. It is widely believed that Israel came into existence as a kind of international reparation for the Holocaust. While this is far from the whole story, it is true that the UN voted in 1947 to partition Palestine into Jewish and Arab states in part to provide a home for Holocaust survivors languishing in displaced persons camps in Europe.

To recast Israeli Jews as the agents of genocide, then, is to reverse the rationale for the country's existence. If the Nakba is like the Holocaust, then Israelis are as bad as Nazis, and their moral claim to their country ought to be revoked.

A striking example of the Holocaust-ification of the Nakba can be found in the 2016 novel *Children of the Ghetto: My Name Is Adam*, by the celebrated Lebanese novelist Elias Khoury. The book is cast as the journal of Adam Dannoun, a Palestinian writer living in New York whose family comes from Lydda, an Arab town near Jerusalem that was conquered by Israel in 1948 and renamed Lod. About 35,000 Arabs were expelled from Lydda in July 1948 and 250 were killed, under circumstances that are disputed by historians. Ari Shavit has written that they were civilians who took refuge in a mosque and were deliberately massacred by Israeli soldiers. Martin Kramer believes there is no evidence of such a massacre, and that most of the Arab dead were soldiers who fell in battle.

For about a month afterwards, as fighting continued in the vicinity, the Arab section of Lydda was fenced off and guarded. The premise of Khoury's novel is that this was the same as what the Jews experienced in the Warsaw Ghetto, where 400,000 Jews were held for two years before being sent to extermination camps. That is the meaning of the novel's title, as Dannoun explains: "I really was a son of the ghetto, and my claims to Polish origins and to being from Warsaw were no more than an appropriate metaphor to describe my childhood in Lydda." He refers to the Arabs conscripted to bury the dead at Lydda as "Sonderkommandos", the term used for Jewish prisoners forced to empty the gas chambers at Auschwitz.

This appropriation of the Holocaust is completely ahistorical. What the Palestinians of Lydda suffered in 1948 and what the Jews suffered in Nazi-occupied Poland are not comparable in severity, in duration or, above all, in motivation. The Nazis killed 6 million Jews because they believed Jews were responsible for all the world's evils and should be erased from the face of the Earth. The Israelis conquered Lydda to open a supply route to Jerusalem, where 100,000 Jews were under an Arab blockade. Yet Khoury insists on the moral equation that he puts in the mouth of Dannoun's Israeli girlfriend: "The Palestinians are the victims of the victims, and the Jewish victims have no right to behave like their executioners." Here is a small but telling example of how genocide becomes a "rhetorical achievement".

The implication of this way of thinking is that Israel's wars, from 1948 down to the present day, are not really wars at all, but episodes in an ongoing Holocaust. This idea helps to explain why the Gaza war is understood in such different terms inside Israel and outside it.

If you talk to Israelis, or pay attention to their press or social media, it is clear they are living in a country at war. They talk about attending shivas for soldiers killed in Gaza, or paying condolence calls on the families of hostages; about their family members who have been called up for military service; about taking shelter during missile attacks. And as in every country that goes to war – even with enemies that are much further away and less directly threatening than Hamas – almost no one has any sympathy to spare for the other side.

After the September 11 attacks, some American experts and intellectuals tried to explain why al-Qaeda was aggrieved by US foreign policy, and warned that invading Afghanistan would cost billions of dollars and tens of thousands of lives without permanently solving any problems. But at a moment of national grief and outrage, such voices were resented and ignored.

In Europe and the US, much of the public does not think of Israel as fighting a war against an enemy

After October 7, Israelis who call attention to the killing of Palestinian women and children, or warn that the ongoing war has done enormous damage to the country's international standing without resolving the future of Gaza, have had an even worse reception. When Amos Schocken, the publisher of the left-leaning newspaper *Ha'aretz*, observed that Israel was "imposing a cruel apartheid regime on the Palestinian population" and referred to Hamas's soldiers as "freedom fighters", he became a national villain and faced reprisals from the Netanyahu government.

In Europe and the United States, however, much of the public does not think of Israel as fighting a war against an enemy. Certainly, Gaza is not discussed in the same way as the war in Ukraine, which has cost about as many civilian lives and vastly more soldiers' lives. This is due to the nature of urban counterterrorist warfare, which cannot be measured in battles won and territory conquered; to the difficulty of independent reporting in the war zone; and to Israel's failure to clearly establish and communicate its objectives.

But it is also because many of the loudest voices on Israel have long believed that the Jewish state's wars are illegitimate by definition, because any attempt to preserve the existence of a criminal country constitutes a crime. Francesca Albanese, the UN special rapporteur on the occupied Palestinian territories, has said repeatedly since October 7 that Hamas has a "right to resist" by attacking Israel, but Israel has no right of self-defence. The supposed legal basis for this idea is that Israel is occupying Gaza in contravention of international law – even though Israel withdrew from Gaza in 2005 and the territory has been governed by Hamas since 2007.

The intellectual basis becomes clear in a report Albanese issued in October 2024, titled "Genocide as Colonial Erasure", which states that, "The violence that Israel has unleashed against the Palestinians post-7 October is not happening in a vacuum, but is part of a long-term intentional, systematic, State-organised forced displacement and replacement of the Palestinians." The report goes on to say that, "Patterns of violence against the group as a whole warrant the application of the Convention on the Prevention and Punishment of the Crime of Genocide (Genocide Convention) in order to cease, prevent and punish genocide in the whole of the occupied Palestinian territory." In other words, the charge of genocide does not apply only to Gaza, where there is an ongoing war, but also to the West Bank, where there is not.

There is no question that Israel has a moral and legal responsibility to investigate the conduct of the war, and punish any soldiers or officers who violated the laws of war. But the evil of war goes beyond the crimes of individuals. War itself is an evil, which can be justified only if it is necessary to prevent worse violence in the future. That is why any country with the means to do so would have responded to a terrorist attack like Hamas's by declaring war. Only in Israel's case is that response construed in terms of genocide. And since the reality of genocide is absent, there have been repeated attempts to invent one.

In December 2023, two months after the start of the war, a food-security non-profit called IPC issued a warning about food scarcity in Gaza. In March 2024, the organisation heightened the alert, declaring that 1.1 million Gazans would begin to starve within a few weeks. When this did not occur, another NGO, the International Food Policy Research Institute, acknowledged that there had been "some improvements in April and May", but warned in June that Gaza again faced "a high risk of famine". Each of these warnings, and others, received enormous publicity as NGOs and the UN repeated the idea that Israel, in the words of Human Rights Watch, had "imposed starvation deadly for children".

By now, a casual reader of the news would surely believe that mass starvation has taken place in the Gaza Strip. This idea fits perfectly into the narrative of genocide, as when *Al Jazeera* reported in an October 2024 article, "Oxfam official tells *Al Jazeera* Israel is using starvation as a weapon in its genocide against the Palestinians." Yet that same article went on to reveal that, a year after the war began, the total number of deaths attributable to malnutrition in Gaza was thirty-seven.

One might think that the non-appearance of a famine that was supposed to kill a million people would be a cause for rejoicing. But of course, that might require re-evaluating the notion that Israel was deploying starvation as a tactic in a genocide against the Palestinians. For many anti-Zionists, the war against Hamas is a genocide for the same reason that the Nakba was a genocide, and every conflict in between: because the existence of a Jewish state itself constitutes a genocidal act against Palestinian Arabs. And since Zionism means supporting the existence of the Jewish state, it follows that Zionists are advocates of genocide, morally equivalent to Nazis.

This has long been a staple of anti-Israel rhetoric in the Arab world. In 2022, Mahmoud Abbas said at a press conference in Berlin that Israel has committed "fifty Holocausts". But it is also taken for granted in much of Western academia. Patrick Wolfe's landmark paper suggests that Zionism is actually worse than Nazism, because "in contrast to the Holocaust", the kind of settler colonialism practised by Israel is "relatively impervious to regime change". The implied logic is that, while Germany could be rescued from Nazism by changing its government – if only at the price of a world war – Israel cannot be rescued from Zionism, since any Israeli government would be committed to preserving the country's identity as a Jewish state. The only solution is to destroy the state itself.

This kind of eliminationist anti-Zionism was extreme when Wolfe wrote in 2006. In the last year, however, it has become conventional wisdom in much of academia and on the left. This became clear in October, when the Palestine Festival of Literature, known as PalFest, announced that thousands of writers had signed on to its boycott of Israel, including Nobel and Pulitzer Prize winners. The signatories agreed not to allow their books to be published in Israel, not to write for Israeli publications and not to participate in readings and conferences in the country. The impetus behind "the largest cultural boycott of Israeli institutions in history", as PalFest proudly called it, was the war in Gaza. But the letter to which so many writers put their names didn't actually call for an end to the war, or for the resignation of Benjamin Netanyahu, or even for Israeli withdrawal from occupied territory in the West Bank. Rather, the letter commits its signatories to avoid working with any Israeli who engages in "whitewashing and justifying Israel's occupation, apartheid or genocide", or who fails to "publicly recognize the inalienable rights of the Palestinian people as enshrined in international law".

It is hard to think of another boycott with demands so far-reaching

This language is deliberately vague, so much so that even some signatories may not fully understand what they are demanding. What does it mean, for instance, to "justify Israel's occupation" of the West Bank? A religious Zionist might justify it on the grounds that the land was promised in the Bible to the descendants of Abraham, Isaac and Jacob forever. A secular Israeli might justify it on the grounds that withdrawing from the West Bank would mean handing it over to a dangerous enemy bent on Israel's destruction – which is what happened when Israel withdrew from Lebanon in 2000 and Gaza in 2005. According to the PalFest letter, both of these positions would be equally unacceptable.

The phrase "the inalienable rights of the Palestinian people" is similarly unclear. Does it mean that the Palestinian people have a right to a state of their own on part of the land between the Jordan River and the Mediterranean Sea? Or does it mean that the descendants of refugees who left or were driven out of Israel in 1948 have a right to return and take back their ancestors' land? In that scenario, Jews would become a minority in the world's twenty-third Arab country. Respecting the "inalienable rights of the Palestinian people", in this view, means that the Jewish state must disappear.

It is hard to think of another boycott with demands so far-reaching. The writers who lent their reputations to this cause are sending a clear message: if you support the existence of a Jewish state in any borders, under any government, you deserve to be treated as a moral pariah. As the thug in the New York subway put it, "We don't want no Zionists here."

3.

That Jews today are being bullied out of public spaces for being Zionists is a terrible historical irony. For the Zionist movement emerged in the 1880s precisely to challenge the exclusion of Jews from the public sphere.

In nineteenth-century Europe, scenes like the one on the New York subway were an inescapable part of Jewish life. A classic example can be found in *The Interpretation of Dreams*, where Sigmund Freud recounts a "youthful experience which, even today, still manifests its power". When he was about ten years old, his father, Jacob, told him about an episode from his own youth, when he was dressed up for Shabbat wearing a new fur cap. A Christian walking by knocked the cap into the mud, shouting, "Jew, get off the sidewalk!" "And what did you do?" the young Sigmund asked. "I went into the street and picked up the cap," Jacob replied. Freud writes that after hearing this story of his father's total helplessness, he began to identify with Hannibal, the ancient Carthaginian general whose father "made his boy swear at the domestic altar to take vengeance on the Romans". Writing decades later, as a grown man, Freud admitted that, "Since that time Hannibal has had a place in my fantasies."

For the founder of psychoanalysis, this was a perfect example of what he called wish fulfilment. In real life, it was impossible for Freud's father to fight back against the Christian, for the same reason that it would have been impossible for a black man in the post–Civil War south to fight back against an insult from a white man: it was simply too dangerous, and not a single institution in society would take his side. Freud himself was unable to fight the antisemitism of the Viennese medical establishment, which held back his career. Instead, his anger and resentment were channelled into his fantasy life, where he identified with Hannibal, the outsider who made the Roman Empire tremble.

At the very moment Freud was writing about this memory, in the 1890s, another Viennese Jew was trying to turn the fantasy into reality. Theodor Herzl was as successfully assimilated as an Austrian Jew could be: he was an editor at the capital's leading newspaper and the author of several successful plays. But he could not escape the knowledge that the Jews of Vienna were humiliatingly vulnerable to Gentile contempt that could erupt at any moment.

Herzl's 1894 play, *The New Ghetto*, tells the story of Jacob Samuel, a Jew who is challenged to a duel by an aristocrat. Initially he declines, but in the end he agrees to fight and is mortally wounded. Carried home to die, he justifies himself to his father: "You will understand, father! You are a man!" To be a man means refusing to be insulted with impunity.

Herzl believed the Jews of his time needed to learn this lesson. In his speculative novel *Old New Land*, he gave Zionism one of its most important slogans: "If you will it, it is no dream." It was an implicit response to Freud: turning Jews from victims into heroes did not have to be a matter of wish fulfilment. "I believe that a wondrous generation of Jews will spring into existence. The Maccabees will rise again," he concluded at the end of "The Jewish State", the 1895 pamphlet that launched the modern Zionist movement. Like the Maccabees of ancient times, Zionism would vindicate Jewish honour by restoring Jewish sovereignty in the land of Israel.

The idea that nationhood requires political existence – that a people cannot flourish unless it has its own state – was, in the late nineteenth century, a progressive belief. The liberal revolutions that spread across Europe in 1848 were called "the springtime of nations" because they saw national liberation as the precondition for individual liberty. In the following decades, Italians and Germans united dozens of feudal principalities into powerful nation-states, while Poles, Czechs, Hungarians and other Eastern European peoples longed to break free from the Russian and Austrian empires.

Again and again, Zionist leaders declared that their goal was to make the Jews a normal nation

In 1862, German philosopher Moses Hess became the first writer to apply this progressive doctrine to the Jews of Europe. In his book *Rome and Jerusalem*, Hess, a one-time collaborator with Karl Marx, wrote that the "resurrection of nations" must include "Israel – the nation which for two thousand years has defied the storms of time". If the Poles and Hungarians deserved nation-states of their own, Hess argued, so did the Jews: "No modern people, struggling for its own fatherland, can deny the right of the Jewish people to its former land, without at the same time undermining its own strivings."

Today, when enemies of Zionism commonly describe it as a form of racism, it is crucial to remember that, for the founders of the Zionist movement, it simply meant equality with other small, oppressed peoples. Again and again, Zionist leaders declared that their goal was to make the Jews a normal nation. Max Nordau, one of Herzl's most important disciples, wrote in 1902 that the Zionist movement's "sole purpose" was "to normalise a people which is living and suffering under abnormal conditions". When Vladimir Jabotinsky, the militant founder of Revisionist Zionism, testified in 1937 before the Peel Commission, which was considering the partition of British Palestine into Arab and Jewish states, he insisted that, "Every nation on Earth, every normal nation … they all have states of their own. That is the normal condition for a people."

If a nation needs a state the way the spirit needs the body, then the Jews were doomed to a spectral existence as long as they remained in the Diaspora. The promise of Zionism was that once a Jewish state came into existence, this abnormality would be cured and other nations would accept the Jewish nation as a peer. As Herzl wrote in his diary in 1895, the goal of Zionism was "that the offensive cry of 'Jew!' may become an honourable appellation, like German, Englishman, Frenchman – in brief, like all civilised peoples".

This language of normalisation concealed what was in fact a revolutionary redefinition of Jewish identity. In modern Central and Western Europe, where Jews had taken seriously the promise of equal citizenship, they did not think of themselves as members of a Jewish people. Rather, they saw Judaism as a religious confession, parallel to Catholicism and Protestantism. Religious identity related to national identity as an adjective to a noun; one could be a German Jew in the same way that others were German Protestants or German Catholics. Under Napoleon, Jews were declared to be no longer tolerated aliens but "Frenchmen of the Mosaic faith".

Zionism made assimilated Jews profoundly uncomfortable because it challenged this way of thinking about Jewishness. The nineteenth century had brought emancipation – the removal of age-old laws that prevented Jews from owning property or holding office, or subjected them to residence restrictions and special taxes. But Zionism insisted that emancipation had not led to true equality and acceptance. On the contrary, it had provoked the rise of a new kind of Jew-hatred, which took the name antisemitism to indicate that it was not merely the same old religious prejudice, but a political ideology.

In the 1890s, this ideology was triumphant in Austria, where Karl Lueger was elected mayor of Vienna under the banner of antisemitism, and in France, where the Dreyfus affair had revealed that half the country supported calls to exterminate the Jews. Herzl, then working as a foreign correspondent in Paris, reported on the 1895 ceremony in which Captain Alfred Dreyfus was stripped of his French military rank after being framed as a spy. In his diary, Herzl wrote that the experience made him recognise "the emptiness and futility of efforts to 'combat antisemitism'".

In *The Jewish State*, written later the same year, he observed that Jews "have honestly endeavoured everywhere to merge ourselves in the social life of surrounding communities and to preserve the faith of our fathers. We are not permitted to do so." The problem, he concluded, was that antisemitism was not a matter of religious bigotry or personal prejudice. It was "a national question, which can only be solved by making it a political world-question".

To resist their enemies, to achieve genuine equality with other peoples, it was necessary for the Jews to forge a political identity. That is perhaps the best definition of Zionism, even today: the belief that whatever else the Jews may be, they are and must be a political community. In Herzl's simple words, "We are a people – one people."

In a sense, the goal of the Zionist movement – the creation of a Jewish state in the Biblical land of Israel – was less important than the existence of the movement itself. The Jewish state that Herzl called for in 1895 would finally be achieved in 1948, after horrors on a scale that the early Zionists, for all their pessimism about the Jewish future in Europe, never imagined. Yet Herzl was correct when he wrote in his diary in 1897, after the First Zionist Congress was held in Switzerland, "At Basel, I founded the Jewish state." He knew that this claim sounded premature: "If I said this out loud today I would be greeted by universal laughter." But he recognised that, simply by beginning to strive for a state, the Zionist movement would make the Jewish people a polity for the first time in 2000 years. And the existence of this polity would one day make a state possible, even necessary.

Herzl insisted in *The Jewish State* that the Zionist project was pragmatic, not utopian. But perhaps the only way a political movement can be born is by underestimating the obstacles in its path; if confronted head-on, they would be too daunting. Herzl believed that it would take just a few years to transfer millions of Jews from Eastern Europe to Palestine, and proposed various legal and financial mechanisms for carrying it out. The main challenge, he believed, was obtaining permission from the Ottoman Empire for the mass settlement of Jews in Palestine. In the few years before his death in 1904, Herzl devoted most of his energy to persuading European governments to back his plan and put diplomatic pressure on the Turkish sultan.

Events proved that he was right about Zionism needing an imperial patron to succeed. But it would not find one until 1917, when Britain conquered Palestine in World War I and promised, in the Balfour Declaration, to make it a "national home for the Jewish people". This was a kind of geopolitical realignment that Herzl could never have achieved on his own. But his successors – notably Chaim Weizmann, the future first president of Israel – were able to seize the opportunity, thanks to the political consciousness and institutions that the Zionist movement had created over the previous two decades.

The Zionists who chose to go to Palestine and stay there were not driven by rational motives: they were political idealists

Still, there were two major obstacles that Zionism failed to reckon with – a failure whose consequences continue to be felt today. The first was the reluctance of Jews to actually move to Palestine in large numbers. Zionism quickly attracted a mass following in Eastern Europe, where the vast majority of Europe's Jews lived in conditions of poverty and persecution far worse than in Vienna or Paris. But most Zionists were content to remain where they were – raising funds, attending meetings, publishing Hebrew newspapers, but in Lvov and Warsaw and Budapest, not in Jaffa or Jerusalem.

S.Y. Agnon, the Nobel Prize–winning Hebrew writer, spoofed this phenomenon in his semi-autobiographical novel *Only Yesterday*, which follows a naive young man named Isaac Kumer in his emigration from Eastern Europe to Ottoman Palestine. At the beginning of the book, Isaac goes to Lvov, the capital of Austrian Galicia, to pay his respects to the famous Zionist leaders he has read about. For their part, these dignitaries are "amazed" to meet someone who is actually on his way to Palestine. "Anyone who is a Zionist and has the wherewithal goes to Conferences; if he's got a lot, he travels to the Congresses," Agnon writes wryly. "In the end, they strayed off into thinking that the end of Zionism is assemblies." These men buy Isaac coffee and cake and send him on his way, saying that one day they might even come to visit him.

In fact, millions of Jews were eager to leave Eastern Europe in this period. It was just that almost any destination appealed to them more than Palestine. Between 1880 and the beginning of World War I in 1914, some 2 million Jews left Eastern Europe for America; only about 75,000 went to Palestine, and many of those left after a few years. (My great-grandfather was one of them. He lived in Palestine during World War I and again in the 1920s, but ended up settling in New York.)

This was entirely rational. People typically emigrate in pursuit of a better life, and as hard as life could be in the Russian Empire, it was even more difficult in this poor, remote corner of the Ottoman

Empire. It follows that the Zionists who chose to go to Palestine and stay there were not driven by rational motives. They were political idealists, mostly young, who were drawn to adventure and sacrifice.

For them, hardship could even be an inducement. Many of the future founders of the State of Israel, including a nineteen-year-old David Ben-Gurion, came to Palestine before World War I as part of the Labor Zionist movement, intent on remaking the character of the Jewish people through arduous farm work. For Aharon David Gordon, the guru of this movement, Zionism meant "our own life feeding on our own vital sources, in the fields and under the skies of our Homeland, a life based on our own physical and mental labours; we want vital energy and spiritual richness from this living source".

But the voluntary mass emigration that Herzl envisioned as the basis of the Jewish state never materialised. Down to the present day, Jews have moved to Israel on a large scale only when driven by crisis. The Jewish population of Israel, which now stands at 7.5 million, is made up not of immigrants but of refugees – from post–World War I Eastern Europe in the 1920s; from Nazi Germany in the 1930s; from Arab countries after the creation of Israel in 1948; and from the Soviet Union after the fall of communism in 1989. There has never been large-scale immigration to Israel from Britain, Australia or France. As for the United States, out of a total Jewish population of 7.5 million, about 2000 to 3000 move to Israel every year – fewer than the number of Israelis who move in the opposite direction. Herzl predicted that antisemitism was the steam that would power the engine of Zionism, and so it has been.

The first great tragedy of Zionism was that at the crucial moment, when the wholesale emigration of European Jewry became both possible and necessary, that engine broke down. In 1937, as the shadows of the Holocaust loomed, Jabotinsky warned that time was running out for the creation of a Jewish state. "We have got to save millions, many millions," he told the Peel Commission. "I do not know whether it is a question of rehousing one-third of the Jewish race, half of the Jewish race or a quarter of the Jewish race; I do not know; but it is a question of millions."

But in 1939, on the eve of World War II, the British government issued a White Paper limiting Jewish immigration to just 75,000 over the next five years. Here was a horribly concrete demonstration of the meaning of statelessness: the Zionist movement, founded to save the Jews of Europe by giving them a Jewish state, had to stand by as they were annihilated. Fury at the British helped give rise to Jewish terrorist groups such as Lehi (an acronym for "Fighters for the Freedom of Israel"), founded in 1940 by Avraham Stern, who believed that Prime Minister Neville Chamberlain was as great an enemy of the Jews as Adolf Hitler.

Eight years later, in April 1948, members of Lehi and the Irgun, a larger and somewhat more moderate terrorist group, killed more than 100 Arabs in the village of Deir Yassin. The massacre became a symbol of the Nakba, and has been invoked ever since – especially during the current war in Gaza – as an example of the supposedly genocidal nature of Zionism. "Israel is guilty of the same massacres and atrocities it has accused Palestinians of committing on October 7," declared an article about Deir Yassin published in *Mondoweiss*.

In this way, Zionism's first unforeseen tragedy – its inability to outrace the Holocaust – turns out to be inextricable from its second – its inability to find a peaceful modus vivendi with the Arabs of Palestine. The decision to shut the doors of Palestine to Jewish refugees in 1939 came after a three-year Arab revolt against Jewish immigration and British rule. Since Britain's global empire included many millions of Arabs and Muslims and almost no Jews, it is not surprising that the British preferred to alienate the latter rather than the former.

The early Zionist movement underestimated the strength and significance of Arab opposition even more dramatically than the danger of European antisemitism. It is often said that the founders of Zionism did not know, or refused to acknowledge, that the land they claimed for a Jewish state was already populated by Arabs.

The first Zionists found it easy to convince themselves that they would be welcomed with open arms

This arrogant ignorance is supposedly encapsulated in a phrase from the British Zionist writer Israel Zangwill, who wrote in 1901 that, "Palestine is a country without a people; the Jews are a people without a country."

In fact, "a land without a people for a people without a land" was never a widespread or official Zionist slogan, and the leaders of the movement – starting with Herzl, who visited Palestine for the first and only time in 1898 – knew perfectly well that Arabs lived there. But they did not reckon with the full implications of this fact. After all, in the 1890s there were no independent Arab states; gaining a foothold in Palestine required persuading the Ottoman sultan, not his Arab subjects. When the British took over the role of imperial overlord, Zionist diplomacy focused on statesmen such as Foreign Secretary Arthur Balfour, the author of the Balfour Declaration.

When the first Zionists did think about what the Arabs would make of Jewish immigration, they found it easy to convince themselves that they would be welcomed with open arms. After all, their purpose in moving to Palestine was not conquest and exploitation, like the European empires engaged in the "scramble for Africa". It was to build a new society that, they believed, would enrich the Arabs as much as the Jews.

In *Old New Land*, Herzl's novel imagining what a Jewish state would look like circa 1923, there is exactly one Arab character, Reschid Bey. When asked by a visiting European, "Don't you regard these Jews as intruders?" he replies indignantly: "Would you call a man a robber who takes nothing from you, but brings you something instead? The Jews have enriched us. Why should we be angry with them? They dwell among us like brothers. Why should we not love them?"

But those on the ground in Ottoman Palestine soon learned better. In 1912, Asher Ginsberg, the leading Zionist writer known by his pen name Ahad Ha'am ("one of the people"), visited Palestine to report on what Zionism had achieved and failed to achieve. He observed that it was already becoming difficult for Jews to purchase land, because "many natives of Palestine, whose national consciousness has begun to develop … look askance, quite naturally, at the selling of land to 'strangers', and do their best to put a stop to this evil".

After the Balfour Declaration, when Jewish immigration began to accelerate, Arab resistance became organised and violent. The Battle of Tel Hai, in 1920, marked the first armed clash in what was to become, by the end of the decade, a de facto civil war between Jews and Arabs. Just thirteen people were killed at Tel Hai, an outpost in what is now northern Israel, where a small number of Jewish soldiers repulsed a larger Arab force. But it looms large in Zionist history, as it marked the first time in 1800 years that a Jewish military fought in defence of the Jewish homeland. Their commander, Joseph Trumpeldor, became the first Jewish military hero since Bar Kochba led a failed rebellion against Roman rule in the second century.

The idea that the Jews would have to win their state by force, fighting a war against both Palestinian Arabs and surrounding Arab states, never entered the dreams of the early Zionists. Yet as we have seen, one of the main goals of the movement was to enable Jews to stand up against their enemies – to put an end to the shame that Freud and Herzl knew so well.

Chaim Nachman Bialik, who died before the State of Israel was founded but is remembered as its national poet and the father of modern Hebrew poetry, captured this shame in a famous poem, "In the City of Slaughter". Written in 1904 in response to a pogrom the previous year in Kishinev, where about fifty Jews were murdered by mobs, the poem is ferociously critical of Jewish men who did not defend themselves against violence. "Descendants of the

Maccabees", Bialik writes, hid from their attackers in privies and pigpens. Instead of taking revenge after the attack, they "fled to the House of the Lord", the synagogue, to ask the rabbi if it was halachically permitted for them to have sex with wives who had been raped.

If, as Herzl promised, the Jewish state was where "the Maccabees will rise again", then one of its purposes must be to teach Jews how to fight. In the 1920s and 1930s, Jabotinsky insisted on this point, recruiting a uniformed youth group he named Betar, after the place where Bar Kochba made his last stand against the Romans. In a 1934 manifesto, Jabotinsky said that members of Betar must learn to use firearms and be ready to "answer personally the call of defence". Beyond that, they must embody the quality of "Hadar", Hebrew for honour or glory, which for Jabotinsky entailed "outward beauty, respect, self-esteem, politeness, faithfulness".

To many Zionists, Betar, with its uniforms and salutes, looked like a Jewish version of the fascist youth militias of Germany and Italy. But Jabotinsky believed that cultivating a Jewish fighting force was a necessity, because despite the pacific visions of mainstream Zionism, Arab opposition to Jewish settlement in Palestine was not going to disappear. In a landmark 1923 essay, "The Iron Wall", he called on the Zionist movement to acknowledge this fact. "It is utterly impossible to obtain the voluntary consent of the Palestine Arabs for converting Palestine from an Arab country into a country with a Jewish majority," he wrote. This was only natural, since every people "regards its lands as its national home, of which it is the sole master, and it wants to retain that mastery always".

If Zionism wanted to create a Jewish state, it could not count on Reschid Bey–like compliance. It would have to overcome Arab opposition by force. Jabotinsky wrote that he did not want to "eject" the Arab population of Palestine, which he considered "utterly impossible". "There will always be two nations in Palestine – which is good enough for me, provided the Jews become the majority," he concluded. But to build that majority, the Jews needed military force as an "iron wall" against Arab opposition. The only question was whether that force would be British, as the Balfour Declaration envisioned and mainstream Zionists accepted, or Jewish, as Jabotinsky and his Revisionist faction preferred.

When Jabotinsky wrote his essay, Palestine was a British colony with a Jewish population of just 85,000 and an Arab population of 650,000. Today Israel controls almost all of the territory

> *"From now on, from the moment we have our own state, you will never be bullied just because you are a Jew"*

between the Jordan River and the Mediterranean Sea, and the Jewish and Arab populations are roughly equal at 7.5 million. In many ways, the dream Herzl described in *Old New Land* has come true. Israel is one of the most prosperous countries in the world, with a per capita GDP nearly equal to that of Britain and France. In 2024, after a year of war, it was ranked the fifth-happiest country in the world by the World Happiness Report, which uses polling and economic data to rank countries on factors including freedom, social support and life expectancy.

Perhaps the most surprising transformation that Zionism wrought in the Jewish people was to make it famous for military prowess – something that would have seemed unimaginable just a century ago, when Jewishness meant powerlessness. Despite its small population, Israel is one of the world's leading military powers, having repeatedly faced down challenges from much larger adversaries. The exploits of its intelligence services and special forces are legendary, from the raid on Entebbe in 1976 to sabotaging the pagers of Hezbollah fighters in 2024.

In his memoir, *A Tale of Love and Darkness*, the great Israeli novelist Amos Oz recalls that the only time he ever saw his father cry was on the night of 29 November 1947, when the United Nations voted to partition British Palestine and create a Jewish state. Oz was born in Jerusalem in 1939 to parents who emigrated from Europe, and on the night of the vote, the whole neighbourhood stayed up to listen to the roll call, which was taking place in New York.

At three or four in the morning, Oz writes, his father, Yehuda – a mild-mannered librarian at the Hebrew University – sat with him in bed and told him, "in a whisper", a story from his own childhood in Vilna. Yehuda was beaten up and had his pants stolen by Gentile boys at school, and when his father went to the school to complain, the same bullies attacked him, "forced him down onto the paving stones in the middle of the playground and removed his trousers too, and the girls laughed and made dirty jokes … while the teachers watched and said nothing, or maybe they were laughing too".

Freud and Herzl and Bialik would have recognised this experience, but Yehuda told the eight-year-old Amos that he never would: "From now on, from the moment we have our own state, you will never be bullied just because you are a Jew ... From tonight that's finished here. Forever."

Yet today, Jews around the world are being insulted and threatened on account of Jewish power, in much the same way that they were once insulted and threatened on account of Jewish powerlessness. In November 2024, Israeli football fans in Amsterdam were set upon in a night of coordinated mass violence that the city's mayor described as a "pogrom". (She later regretted using the word, saying it had been "politicised".) The following month, arsonists burned down a synagogue in Melbourne.

Such attacks are the natural sequel to the spread of anti-Zionist rhetoric that casts the Jewish state, its citizens and its supporters as genocidal sadists. More than a century ago, Zionism allowed the Jewish people to enter the public sphere – first as a political community, then as a sovereign state. Attempts to destroy the state by military force have been thwarted one after another, from the 1948 war to the decimation of Lebanese Hezbollah last year. Now anti-Zionism hopes to achieve what force could not, by revoking the political existence of the Jewish people, which is the precondition for the state's existence. On a New York subway carriage or the floor of the UN General Assembly, anti-Zionists want to convince the world – and, even more importantly, Jews themselves – that they have no right to exist in public space.

4.

A century after it was written, *The Iron Wall* remains the most important text for understanding Zionism, because it made the cost of a Jewish state explicit. The moment the Jewish people began to work for the creation of a state in their Biblical homeland, they put themselves on a collision course with the Arabs living there. The iron wall that Jabotinsky saw as a temporary necessity, until the Arabs agreed to accept minority status in a Jewish state, has proved to be a permanent feature of Israeli life, and in many ways the defining one. For Jews, the iron wall means compulsory military service and the Iron Dome and basement bomb shelters. For Palestinians in the West Bank, it means security fences and road checkpoints and house demolitions; for Palestinians in Gaza over the last year, it has meant forced evacuations and artillery shelling and air strikes.

Clearly those who live inside the iron wall are better off than those outside, but both peoples are living in its shadow. And this shadowed existence is not the "normal" life that Zionism hoped to achieve for the Jewish people. More than seventy-five years after Israel was founded, it has no agreed-upon borders and no diplomatic recognition from most of its regional neighbours. The Jewish majority that Jabotinsky saw as indispensable does not exist "between the river and sea", so the Jewish character of the state can be maintained only by denying citizenship to Arabs in the West Bank.

The sense that Israel is still provisional, an experiment rather than an accomplished fact, is one thing Israelis and Palestinians have in common. In May 2023, the seventy-fifth anniversary of Israel's founding and of the Nakba, a survey conducted by the Palestinian Center for Policy and Survey Research found that 66 per cent of Palestinians believed Israel would not survive to 100. At the same time, a poll by the *Times of Israel* found that 51 per cent of Israelis were pessimistic about the country's future. A poll conducted a year earlier found that 33 per cent of Israelis had considered emigrating; for people aged eighteen to twenty-four, the figure was 66 per cent.

In this situation, Israel's military strength is proportional to its existential weakness. It is a vicious circle: Israel never feels secure enough to stop exercising force and it can never exercise enough force to make itself secure. That is how a country that perceives itself as highly vulnerable and encircled by enemies comes to be seen by much of the world as callously, oppressively strong. This

> *Clearly those who live inside the iron wall are better off than those outside, but both peoples are living in its shadow*

dynamic was on display when the International Criminal Court issued an arrest warrant for Prime Minister Benjamin Netanyahu and Defence Minister Yoav Gallant on charges of war crimes. For the court, as for many people around the world, Netanyahu was a cruel warmonger; for Netanyahu, as for many people in Israel, the court was "antisemitic from beginning to end", the latest in a long line of enemies of the Jewish people.

The psychic cost of living inside an iron wall is one of the major themes of Israeli literature. Amos Oz – who exchanged his family name, Klausner, for the Hebrew word for "strength" – dramatised it in his first book, *Where the Jackals Howl*, published in 1965. A collection of stories inspired by Oz's life on a kibbutz, the book takes its title from the eerie sound of the animals just outside the borders of the settlement: "Beyond the fence lived another world, which silently yearned by day and night to raze the house to the ground, gnawing slyly and with infinite patience."

For Oz, this hostile force represents not just the Arabs, who used to live on the land where the kibbutz now stands, but the unconscious desires of the kibbutzniks themselves, which have to be repressed in the name of unity and security. The psychic cost of living the Zionist dream is all too clear in the story "The Way of the Wind", about a young paratrooper named Gideon who has grown up in the shadow of his father, a stern Zionist pioneer. When Gideon's unit makes a jump near his home, he pulls the cord of his emergency parachute as well as his main chute, hoping to make himself conspicuous so his father will see him. But the added lift makes him drift off course and get caught on a power line, where he is electrocuted. In trying to prove how brave he is, he ends up killing himself.

Zionist strength is even more troubling in David Grossman's 2008 novel, *To the End of the Land*, in which a mother named Ora flees her house so as not to receive the notification of her son Ofer's death in combat, which she fears will arrive at any moment. Her protective love is complicated by the knowledge that, on an earlier tour of duty, Ofer helped his comrades torture a Palestinian prisoner, leaving him in a meat locker for two days. She can hardly understand how the boy she raised could be capable of such cruelty.

Grossman helps to explain it by narrating an incident from Ofer's childhood, when he became obsessed with the idea that an Arab was trying to kill him and take his room – a childlike interpretation of the Arab–Israeli conflict. To dispel his fears, Ora took the young boy to the tank museum at Latrun, where he saw "dozens of tanks, both ancient and new". "Is this ours?" Ofer asks, and his mother tells him, "Yes, and there's lots more. We have loads of these." The boy is reassured to see that he and his country are not defenceless, that they can fight back against their enemies, and his fears go away.

"At the time," Ora reflects, "I thought that what was good enough for a whole country was good enough for my child." After all, that is the point of the Israel Defense Forces – to reassure the nation that they can fight back against their enemies. But in teaching Ofer to take pride in military strength, did she plant the seeds that would later lead him to use his own strength brutally and unjustly?

That question, too, applies to the whole country. The Hamas attack on October 7 was Israel's deepest nightmare come to life: all its strength could not stop its enemies from massacring 1,200 people, considerably more than were killed during the Six-Day War. The attack has been frequently described as the worst mass killing of Jews since the Holocaust – a comparison that tells us less about October 7 than about how close to the surface the Jewish fear of annihilation remains, in Israel and around the world. So it was all too predictable, when Israel retaliated against Hamas in Gaza, that fear and helplessness would give rise to vengeance.

The tone was set by Yoav Gallant when he announced, two days after the attack, "We are fighting human animals and we are acting accordingly." What that meant in practice is clear from *Ha'aretz's* December 2024 report on the Netzarim corridor, which bisects the Gaza Strip. IDF soldiers testified that it was unofficial policy to shoot any Palestinian who crossed an unmarked boundary line and count them as a terrorist in official death tolls. Out of 200 people killed, only ten turned out to be actual Hamas fighters.

No doubt similar stories will emerge when the war is over. Moshe Ya'alon, a former defence minister and long-time critic of Netanyahu, said in late November, "War crimes are being committed here." Israeli soldiers have posted videos of themselves on social media celebrating the destruction of Palestinian homes and mocking and threatening prisoners. The IDF has condemned such videos as "deplorable" and denied that they represent the military at large, but they have done incalculable damage to Israel's reputation, especially among young people who get most of their news from social media.

In *The Iron Wall*, Jabotinsky wrote that the Arabs of Palestine would never agree to the creation of a Jewish state, "so that all those who regard such an agreement as a condition sine qua non for Zionism may as well say 'non' and withdraw from Zionism". He turned out to be right that the only way to create a Jewish state was by force of arms. A century later, however, it is clear that creating the state was only the beginning. It has been far more costly, materially and morally, to keep manning the iron wall through generations of war and occupation, in which Israelis continue to suffer and inflict evils.

No wonder that some Jews have concluded that the price is too high and taken up Jabotinsky's suggestion of withdrawing from Zionism. Only a small fraction of Jews describe themselves as anti-Zionist, even after a year of war in Gaza. (In June 2024, the American Jewish Committee's public opinion survey found that 45 per cent of American Jews felt more closely connected to Israel since October 7, compared with 19 per cent who felt less connected.) But anti-Zionist Jewish figures such as Judith Butler, Naomi Klein and Peter Beinart have made highly visible arguments, not just against the actions of the Israeli government and military, but against the existence of Israel itself.

At a time when Israel and Zionism are under attack, many Jews see such critics as traitors, or useful idiots for the enemy, and dismiss them accordingly. The American Jewish Committee put out a list of talking points, "What You Need to Know About Anti-Zionist Jews", explaining that, "Anti-Zionist Jews are often used as cover by extremist groups to 'kosher' their antisemitic messaging." In May 2024, *Commentary* magazine published an article on "The Shameful History of Anti-Zionist Jews", asking scornfully, "Who are these people? What is motivating such thinking, such talk, such bile?" Elliott Abrams, a veteran American diplomat, wrote an essay in *Fathom Journal* denouncing "the Naomi Kleins and the Peter Beinarts and the hundreds of Jewish professors who wish to proclaim their virtue by lining up against the Jewish State".

> *Attacking a critic's motives leaves the impression that one is unable to deal with their arguments*

But it is a mistake to dismiss thoughtful anti-Zionist Jews in this way. For one thing, accusing them of caring too much about virtue risks implying that Zionist Jews don't care enough about it. And attacking a critic's motives leaves the impression that one is unable to deal with their arguments.

In the Arab world and among doctrinaire progressives, hostility to Israel is a given. But Jews who become anti-Zionists usually started out as Zionists, or were raised in communities where the goodness of Zionism and Israel was taken for granted. Sometimes this community was Israel itself. The historian Ilan Pappé, who was born in Haifa in 1954 and served in the Yom Kippur War, was one of the leading figures in the "post-Zionist" movement of the 1990s, in which Israeli academics and artists attempted to dismantle what they saw as the myths that sustained the Jewish state. Pappé writes in *The Idea of Israel* that some Israelis "leave the tribe of Zionism because you witnessed an event conducted in the name of Zionism that was so abhorrent it made you rethink the validity of the ideology that licensed such brutality".

He gives several examples of such anti-Zionist "trailblazers". The poet Maxim Ghilan was arrested in 1950 as a member of the ultra-nationalist Lehi but turned against Zionism when he witnessed Arab fellow prisoners being tortured. The journalist Boaz Evron, whose great-grandfather had been one of the first Zionist settlers in Palestine, became an anti-Zionist after hearing an Israeli soldier describe how he and his comrades tear-gassed a classroom full of young Palestinian boys. Yeshayahu Leibowitz, the Orthodox intellectual who famously warned that the occupation was turning

Israelis into "Judeo-Nazis", was radicalised by the Qibya massacre in 1953, when Israeli soldiers commanded by future prime minister Ariel Sharon killed more than sixty Palestinian civilians in a West Bank village, in retaliation for a Palestinian raid that had killed an Israeli mother and her two children.

Over decades of war and occupation, many anti-Zionists have had similar stories to tell. The historian Daniel Boyarin, born in New Jersey, made *aliyah* and raised his family in Israel, but left after twenty years "when I heard Yitzhak Rabin say that the breaking of the arms and legs of children throwing stones was necessary to preserve the state", he writes in his book *The No-State Solution*. Shaul Magid, an American-born rabbi and academic, writes in *The Necessity of Exile*, "I did not lose my Zionism in left-wing protests. I lost my Zionism in the IDF," while serving a tour of duty in the occupied West Bank. The war in Gaza is sure to produce more such stories.

No one with a functioning conscience could fail to share these writers' revulsion against cruelty and violence. Their stories confirm that war and occupation are dehumanising, not only for the defeated and the imprisoned, but for the victor and the occupier as well.

Yet wars continue to be fought, because sometimes they are necessary evils. Peoples have fought to liberate themselves from foreign domination, as in Vietnam and Algeria after World War II, or to preserve their independence, as in Ukraine today. Those conflicts and many others produced stories as terrible as the ones told by Pappé's "trailblazers", and far more numerous. But there is only one case in which a country's critics, internal and external, believe that because "abhorrent" acts have been committed "in its name", it should cease to exist.

It is instructive to compare the history of Israel since 1948 with those of India and Pakistan, which were created in 1947 under similar circumstances – British withdrawal followed by civil war. In the first months after the partition of India and Pakistan, fighting between Hindus and Muslims killed up to 2 million people, while driving 15 million into exile. When Bengalis who had been incorporated into East Pakistan seceded to form Bangladesh in 1971, the ensuing war killed up to 3 million people. The border between India and Pakistan is still disputed today, more than seventy-five years after partition, and border skirmishes and terrorist attacks are regular occurrences. Yet when was the last time you heard someone say that India or Pakistan shouldn't exist?

Since I am an American, let me take an example closer to home. After the September 11 attacks, the United States retaliated by invading first Afghanistan, where Osama bin Laden had his base of operations, and then Iraq, which had nothing to do with September 11 or al-Qaeda but was a longstanding American adversary. In April 2004, it was reported that American soldiers at the Abu Ghraib prison in Baghdad had tortured and sexually humiliated Iraqi prisoners. Photographs taken by the torturers became infamous around the world. In one, a hooded man is forced to stand on a narrow box while he receives electric shocks through wires attached to his fingertips. In another, a female soldier holds a leash attached to the neck of a naked man, who was ordered to lie on the ground and bark like a dog.

These revelations did huge damage to the reputation of the United States around the world. But they did not stop George W. Bush from being re-elected as president in 2004, or bring an end to the American occupation of Iraq, which lasted until 2011, or of Afghanistan, which lasted until 2021. Nor, of course, did they lead anyone to say that the American Revolution had been a mistake and the United States should be dissolved.

Such comparisons suggest that what is unique about Israel is neither its history nor its conduct, but the widespread belief that its sovereignty is conditional. Jewish anti-Zionists contribute to this belief by viewing statehood as a historical experiment that the Jewish people has failed. Ironically, their definition of failure is exactly the same as the early Zionists' definition of success: becoming normal.

Beinart is not the only Jewish intellectual to suggest that exile is better for Jews and Judaism than statehood

For a normal state commits injustices that a stateless people cannot. As Magid writes, by seeing "the Jews as simply a nation among nations", Zionist "normalization seeks to erase the exilic and thus 'abnormal' quality of the Jewish people which had historically prevented them from enacting the same national pursuits as other nations" – pursuits including war and chauvinism.

If Jewish political existence means sinking to the level of the "normal" state, anti-Zionists feel, then it is not worth the price. Better to return to the condition of exile, in which powerlessness to prevent evil went hand in hand with powerlessness to commit it.

In his 2020 essay "Yavne: A Jewish Case for Equality in Israel-Palestine", the American journalist Peter Beinart argues that it was not important for Jews to have a state in the land of Israel; all they need is a "home", which need not take political form. The Talmud relates that when Jerusalem was besieged by the Romans, in the first century CE, the rabbinic sage Yochanan ben Zakkai escaped from the doomed city and begged the emperor Vespasian for a favour: "Give me Yavne and its sages." After Jerusalem and Judea were destroyed, Yochanan and his disciples enabled Judaism to survive by creating an academy in the town of Yavne, where they turned a Temple-based religion of sacrifice into a diasporic religion centred on law and study.

By invoking Yavne, Beinart suggests that the fall of the State of Israel is not to be feared. Judaism can learn to survive without a Jewish state just as it once learned to survive without a Temple. In 70 CE, he writes, "A phase of Jewish history had run its course. It was time for Jews to imagine a different path. That time has come again."

Beinart is not the only Jewish intellectual to suggest that exile is better for Jews and Judaism than statehood. Magid finds inspiration in Hasidic thinkers who "felt that the messianic era could not commence until the exile had been adequately experienced". Judith Butler writes that, "Jewish values of cohabitation with the non-Jew … are part of the very ethical substance of diasporic Jewishness", where "commitments to social equality and social justice have been an integral part of Jewish secular, socialist, and religious traditions". And Daniel Boyarin rejects Zionism in favour of a "diasporic nationalism that offers not the promise of security, but rather the highly contingent possibility of an ethical collective existence".

These anti-Zionist intellectuals can point to distinguished predecessors, going all the way back to the prophet Samuel, who rebuked the Israelites for demanding a king so that "we may be like all the other nations". For Isaac Bashevis Singer, the true spirit of Judaism was found in the Yiddish language, which – he said in his 1978 Nobel lecture – possesses "no words for weapons, ammunition, military exercises, war tactics". It could do without such terms because it was "a language of exile, without a land, without frontiers, not supported by any government". The clear contrast, of course, is with modern Hebrew, which does not enjoy the privilege of powerlessness.

But the figure most often invoked by Jewish opponents of Jewish statehood is Ahad Ha'am, the founder of "cultural Zionism". While Theodor Herzl and other early Zionists focused on politics and diplomacy, Ahad Ha'am believed that the most urgent tasks for the Zionist movement were spiritual and cultural. Rather than a Jewish state, he argued, Zionists should work to create a Jewish centre in Palestine as a source of inspiration for Jews around the globe. Beinart's distinction between a "home" and a "state" is very much in this tradition. In 2020, he told an interviewer, "I believe that a Jewish society in the land of Israel is deeply important. In that way, I'm influenced by people like Ahad Ha'am."

In their eagerness to claim Ahad Ha'am as one of their own, however, today's anti-Zionists often distort his ideas. For one thing, he was a Zionist from beginning to end – not an opponent of Jewish nationalism, but a champion of it. Much of his criticism of "political Zionism", the approach associated with Herzl, grew out of his pessimism about what it could accomplish. He believed Zionism should not define itself primarily as a political movement because "if the political ideal is not attained, it will have disastrous consequences". After attending the First Zionist Congress in 1897, where Herzl claimed to have founded the Jewish state, Ahad Ha'am warned that "the enthusiasm is artificial, and in the end it will lead to the despair that follows disillusionment".

This does not mean he opposed the goal of a Jewish state. Rather, he believed that Zionism should focus first on building the foundation for a state – both the economic and social infrastructure needed in Palestine, and the national consciousness needed to unite Jews in the Diaspora. He called for "the strengthening of our national unity by joint action in every sphere of our national life, until we become capable and worthy of a life of dignity and freedom *at some time in the future*".

It was one thing to say in 1897 that a Jewish state was premature; it is quite another to say in 2025 that a Jewish state that has existed for more than seventy-five years, and is home to 7.5 million Jews, should be abandoned. There is almost no support for this position among the Jewish public, in Israel or abroad, yet it has a curious appeal for intellectuals, just as earlier generations of Jewish intellectuals such as Hannah Arendt and Judah Magnes hoped to create a binational state in Palestine.

Anti-Zionist Jews deny that the disappearance of Israel would be dangerous for Israeli Jews. But it is difficult to understand why

Jews and Arabs, who have spent generations inflicting terrible injuries on one another, would suddenly lie down together like the lion and the lamb if placed under a single government. Beinart writes that a binational Israel-Palestine could resemble Belgium, where Flemings and Walloons have settled into a grudging but non-violent coexistence. But it is far more likely that it would resemble Israel's actual neighbours, Syria, Lebanon and Iraq, where attempts to unite Sunnis and Shias, Muslims and Christians, Arabs and Kurds, have led to catastrophe.

If Zionism created Jewish politics, it is not surprising that anti-Zionism abolishes the ability to think clearly about politics. In arguing that exile is better for the Jews than statehood – even

Anti-Zionist thinkers blind themselves to what Jewish powerlessness looked like in the past

that "dispersion is the mode in which Jews have in fact survived", as Judith Butler writes – anti-Zionist thinkers blind themselves to what the transition from Israel to not-Israel would actually look like, just as they blind themselves to what Jewish powerlessness looked like in the past.

Those who long to return to the cultural Zionism of Ahad Ha'am forget the reason why that tradition died out in the first place: because the Holocaust showed that the Jewish people could not afford to wait until "some point in the future" to create a state. They needed a country where they could defend themselves, and where no imperial overlord or hostile neighbour could shut the doors to desperate refugees.

In the same way, Beinart's praise of Yavne ignores the reality behind it. "When Rabbi Yochanan ben Zakkai asked the Roman Emperor to give him Yavne, he was acknowledging that a phase of Jewish history had run its course," Beinart writes. But it was not that a phase had "run its course"; it was that the Romans had killed Jews on a scale not to be exceeded until the Holocaust 2000 years later. According to the historian Josephus, who was a commander in the Jewish forces, the siege of Jerusalem killed 1.1 million civilians, mostly by famine. By the end, he writes, there was no "place in the city that had no dead bodies in it, but what was entirely covered with those that were killed either by the famine or the rebellion".

This, and many scenes like it in later generations, is the reality of Jewish powerlessness, which Boyarin praises for offering "the possibility of an ethical collective existence". As for the notion that a powerless people is more ethical than a secure one, reading Josephus dispels that fantasy as well. In besieged Jerusalem, mothers ate their dead children. The truth is just the opposite: it is only when a people has power over its own destiny that it can be held ethically responsible, or found guilty of irresponsibility.

In renouncing these lessons of Zionism, anti-Zionists are reverting to a way of thinking about power and sovereignty with deep roots in Jewish tradition. After all, the idea that Jewish sovereignty in the land of Israel is conditional, and can be revoked as punishment at any moment, is exactly what Moses told the Israelites when they were about to cross the Jordan. Even before they claimed the land, Moses promised the people that one day they would forfeit it:

And later generations will ask – the children who succeed you, and foreigners who come from distant lands and see the plagues and diseases that the Lord has inflicted upon that land … "Why did the Lord do thus to this land? Wherefore that awful wrath?" They will be told, "Because they forsook the covenant that the Lord, God of their ancestors, made with them upon freeing them from the land of Egypt." (Deuteronomy 29:21–24).

But the Bible is equally clear that the Jewish people cannot reject the trial of sovereignty. Moses's warning didn't stop Joshua from leading the Israelites into the Promised Land, just as Samuel's warning didn't stop Saul from being anointed as Israel's first king. Of course, the Torah says that there were some Israelites who wanted to return to Egypt rather than go forward into Canaan. We may have been slaves, they complained to Moses, but at least "we sat by the fleshpots, we ate our fill of bread". Perhaps a few also argued that it is easier for a slave to be innocent than for a free man to be good. But it was only by crossing the desert and entering the Promised Land that the Israelites could reach the age of Solomon, when "Judah and Israel from Dan to Beersheba dwelt in safety, every family under its own vine and fig tree" (1 Kings 5:5).

5.

Zionism was a movement to create a Jewish state. Logically speaking, it should have disappeared in 1948, the way scaffolding is dismantled after the building is complete. So why is it still needed in 2025?

The answer has to do with Israel's central strategic failure, which threatens to undo all its tactical victories: its inability to reconcile the Palestinian Arabs to its existence.

When David Ben-Gurion and other leaders issued Israel's Declaration of Independence, on 15 May 1948, they included two appeals, "in the very midst of the onslaught launched against us now for months". One was addressed "to the Arab inhabitants of the State of Israel to preserve peace and participate in the upbuilding of the State", the other to "all neighbouring states and their peoples in an offer of peace and good neighbourliness". These appeals were ignored in favour of war, which Israel won, at the cost of some 6000 lives – about 1 per cent of the new nation's Jewish population.

After several decades and several more wars, Israel's neighbouring states abandoned the effort to destroy it. The Arab citizens of Israel, too, are for the most part peaceful participants in the life of the country. But for the majority of Palestinian Arabs displaced in 1948 and brought under Israeli occupation in 1967, the existence of a Jewish state remains at best an insult to tolerate, at worst an injury to avenge.

Between 2014 and 2020, the Washington Institute for Near East Policy conducted a series of public opinion polls in the West Bank and Gaza, asking whether "to end the occupation, the Palestinians should accept the principle of 'two states for two peoples – the Palestinian people and the Jewish people'", or reject it, "because we should not accept a state for the Jewish people". In every year but one, the majority of Palestinians rejected it – in 2020, by a margin of 68 per cent to 32 per cent.

That enduring consensus explains why Palestinian leaders have refused every offer to partition the land "between the river and sea", from the Peel Commission in 1937 to Camp David in 2000. It is why UNRWA continues to designate as refugees the grandchildren and great-grandchildren of Palestinians who left Israel more than seventy years ago. It is one reason why Egypt refused to open its border to allow Palestinian civilians to flee Israel's campaign against Hamas, the way Turkey welcomed millions of Syrians during that country's civil war.

It is also why Hamas attacked Israel on October 7 and held civilian hostages, despite knowing what kind of retaliation would ensue. "Today, the enemy has had a political, military, intelligence, security and moral defeat inflicted upon it, and we shall

Zionism is simply the belief that a Jewish state is necessary for the survival and wellbeing of the Jewish people

crown it, with the grace of God, with a crushing defeat that will expel it from our lands," said Hamas leader Ismail Haniyeh on October 7. To expel the Jews, any price was worth paying. (Haniyeh himself was killed by Israel in Iran in July 2024.)

Despite the dreams of the left in the 1990s, Israelis have not been able to end the Palestinian conflict with territorial concessions. Despite the dreams of the far right today, they have never been brutal enough to end it with expulsion. Instead, under the leadership of Ariel Sharon and Benjamin Netanyahu, for two decades Israel dominated the Palestinians so thoroughly that it could afford to keep deferring the primary, existential question: is the Jewish state an accomplished fact? Or is it still a proposition, one that must be defended physically, politically and morally, day after day, year after year?

October 7 and its aftermath left no doubt of the answer. Much of the world has taken the Israel–Hamas conflict as an occasion to renew the case against Israel's existence – and young people in the West are increasingly receptive. In Britain, a June 2024 poll found that 54 per cent of people aged eighteen to twenty-four agreed with the statement, "Israel should not exist." In Canada, support for Hamas in its war with Israel was almost non-existent among people over fifty-five, but those aged eighteen to twenty-four supported Hamas over Israel by a two-to-one margin.

Political ideologies often find themselves in the position of winning in theory but losing in practice. In the twentieth century, much of the world embraced the belief that communism was the best way to organise society, even as actual communist societies turned into famine-stricken dictatorships. Zionism is the rare exception: an idea that succeeded in practice while remaining fiercely contested in theory. It created a Jewish state but has not convinced the world of the state's legitimacy and permanence – what Israel's Declaration of Independence called "the natural right of the Jewish people to be masters of their own fate, like all other nations, in their own sovereign State".

Zionism isn't the only long-established political idea under attack today. Over the last decade, the Western liberal order has been challenged from within and without. Most of its defenders have responded by insisting that criticism of things like free speech and free trade, the European Union and NATO, is simply impermissible, out of bounds. This strategy has failed to halt the rise of populism, nativism and isolationism, and it cannot halt the rise of anti-Zionism either. Rather, when an idea is challenged, those who believe in it must be able to mount a substantive defence – to show why it is as worthy and necessary today as it was a generation or a century ago.

For Zionists, that means reclaiming the definition of the word from its opponents. Zionism has nothing to do with "creating a racist hierarchy with European Jews at the top", as Jewish Voice for Peace says, or a "chronic addiction to territorial expansion", in the words of Patrick Wolfe. Today, as when it began, Zionism is simply the belief that a Jewish state is necessary for the survival and well-being of the Jewish people.

Since the 1890s, Zionists have disagreed about every aspect of that state. Should it be in the land of Israel or somewhere else? Should its people speak a European language or Hebrew? Should its laws be religious or secular? What relationship should it have with Jews who live in other countries and non-Jews who live inside its borders? Where should its borders be drawn? Some of those debates were resolved long ago, others are still going on today. But they are all internal to Zionism, because they all begin from the principle that the Jewish people needs a Jewish state.

That Israel is needed for Jewish survival has been too amply and terribly vindicated to need rehearsing. It is demonstrated in the story of the *St Louis*, a ship that departed Nazi Germany in May

1939 carrying almost 1000 Jewish refugees. On arriving in Cuba, the passengers were refused permission to come ashore; then they were denied entry to the United States and Canada. They had no choice but to return to Europe, and all those who failed to find another way out were killed in the Holocaust. The right of return, which guarantees Israeli citizenship to all Jews who ask for it, is often attacked by anti-Zionists as an example of ethnocentrism. In fact, it is a simple necessity: as long as there is a Jewish state, there will not be another story like the *St Louis*.

The argument that Israel is indispensable to Jewish wellbeing is more complicated, because it requires asking what it means for a people to flourish. Ahad Ha'am hoped that Jewish Palestine would serve this purpose by becoming a kind of social laboratory where "bodily work and spiritual purification" would create perfect Jews, "a true miniature of the people of Israel as it ought to be". He looked forward to the day when people would say, "If you wish to see the genuine type of a Jew, whether it be a Rabbi or a scholar or a writer, a farmer or an artist or a business man – then go to Palestine, and you will see it."

This vision has not come to pass. Israel is important to Jews around the world, but not because they see Israelis as the best or most genuine Jews. From Chabad headquarters in Brooklyn to Reform synagogues in Hampstead or St Kilda, the Diaspora offers many ways to live a Jewish life that are not possible in Israel. Ahad Ha'am's twenty-first-century admirers might say this is because Israel went astray. It failed to become a "national spiritual centre" because it sought power instead of purification.

What the history of Israel really shows, however, is that any people can be "as it ought to be" only in the imagination, in visions of the future. Any actually existing people will fall short of this ideal. The Bible makes clear that the Jewish people are no exception: from the Golden Calf to the Babylonian exile, the Israelites fail God again and again. The rabbis of the Talmud say God gave the Jews a "fiery law", full of onerous restrictions and punishments, because nothing less could discipline a "fiery people". "For what reason was the Torah given to the Jewish people? It is because they are impudent," Rabbi Meir explained. Surely every prophet and lawgiver would say the same about his all-too-human followers.

The real transformation that Zionism has wrought is not moral, spiritual or cultural, but political. In the State of Israel, Jews have more control over their own destiny than any Jewish community in at least 2000 years. And while

It is Jews outside Israel who face pressure to defend their Zionism, or else renounce it

"Hatikvah", the Israeli national anthem, declares "the hope" of the Jews "to be a free people in our land", the existence of Israel has made Jews more free in other lands, too. Jewish political existence means that being a Jew is a valid public identity, rather than what it was for most of history – a handicap that must be overcome in order to win membership to another, more legitimate, group. It means that Jews have the right to exist on our own account, and not by the grace and favour of an outside authority, which might be revoked at any moment.

These may sound like abstract benefits when weighed against the concrete hostility of anti-Zionism. For some Jews today, who have never lived in a world without a Jewish state, it can seem that since the only hostility they face on account of being Jewish comes from critics of Israel, the natural solution is to get rid of Israel. Surely then the Jews would have no enemies! This is the same kind of logic that leads people to call for the abolition of the polio vaccine because they're afraid vaccines can have side effects – and after all, they've never met anyone with polio.

The combination of Zionist freedom and American freedom has allowed me to live my entire life without feeling ashamed or afraid because I am a Jew. The more I learn about Jewish history, and Jewish literature, the more I realise how rare a privilege that has been. Now it often feels like that privilege is slipping away – that "the golden age of American Jewry is ending", as the American journalist Franklin Foer wrote in a much-discussed essay in *The Atlantic*.

This feeling is surely connected with the end of the golden age of America itself. But it also has to do with the precipitous rise of anti-Zionism, which wants to bring back Jewish shame and fear in new forms. Instead of being ashamed and afraid because we have no power, anti-Zionism wants us to be ashamed that the State of Israel has too much power, and afraid that any Jew anywhere might be punished for it.

A childhood friend of mine from Los Angeles, who has lived in Jerusalem for twenty years and raised a family there, surprised me recently by saying that she thought that since October 7, American Jews have had a harder time than Israeli Jews. At first I couldn't understand it: whatever social and political pressure we've encountered in the US is surely insignificant compared to Hezbollah rockets and Iranian drones. But when it comes to psychology, perhaps my friend had a point. Israelis, being fully engaged in defending their country's existence with arms, are not very troubled by demands to defend its right to exist with words. It is Jews outside Israel who face pressure to defend their Zionism, or else renounce it. Many of us now feel conspicuous and vulnerable in places where we were once at ease, from synagogues to college campuses. Indeed, it has been surprising to see how vulnerable even the most successful and well-integrated Jewish communities feel. Immediately after October 7, I heard lawyers and professors and tech executives compare America to Germany in January 1933 and talk about buying guns to defend their homes.

This kind of atavistic fear should not cause the Jewish people to forget the political lessons we have learned over the last century and a half. The most important of those lessons is that fear attracts enemies and confidence deters them. Instead of treating anti-Zionism as a new kind of antisemitism and demanding that the world protect us against it, then, we should recognise it as an attack on Jewish political existence and respond politically.

That means publicly affirming the justice and necessity of a Jewish state. The reasons that inspired the Zionist movement to create Israel, and the UN to recognise it, are no less valid today than in the past. The survival of Israel as a Jewish state is an existential necessity for the millions of Jews living there and millions living elsewhere. Contrary to the fantasies of anti-Zionists, there is no way it could cease to exist without massive violence. The October 7 attack was a clear preview of what "liberating Palestine" means to Hamas and other militant groups. With the Holocaust still in living memory, it is unthinkable that Israeli Jews would give up the security of their own state and military, and unthinkable for other people, Jews or non-Jews, to ask them to.

In making this case, Zionists must refuse to be intimidated by hostile words or even actions. Courage belongs to the essence of Zionism, and Jews in Israel have to display it every day, not only soldiers but civilians as well. In Western countries, where Jews face hostility in certain milieus but actual violence is very rare, there is no excuse for panic.

One way of being intimidated is refusing to acknowledge when Israel does wrong, for fear of giving aid to its enemies. That fear, too, must be resisted. If Israelis are not afraid to protest their government's actions, Jews outside Israel should not be afraid to listen to them. Indeed, steadfast commitment to the existence of Israel is what makes honest criticism of it possible. Both are required if Zionism is to address its greatest unfinished task: securing the future of the Jewish state by finally making a lasting peace between Jews and Arabs. ▤

Past issues

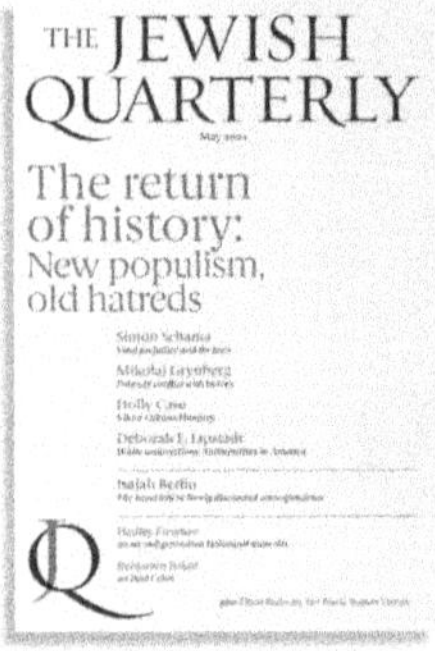
THE JEWISH QUARTERLY
The return of history:
New populism, old hatreds

"For a long time now, the authority of knowledge has been under siege from those who march under the banner of pure belief." —Simon Schama

The Return of History investigates rising global populism, and the forces propelling modern nativism and xenophobia.

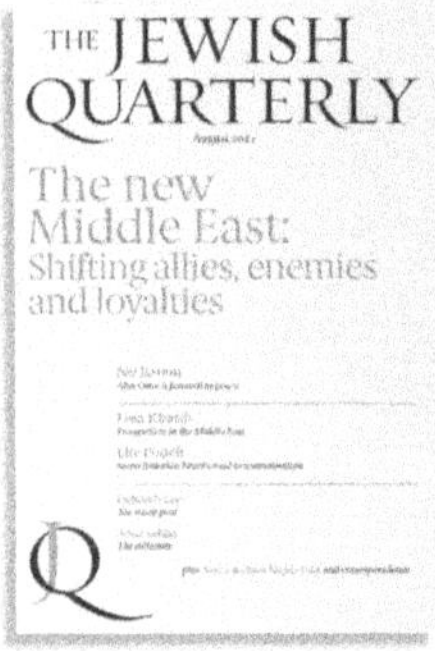
THE JEWISH QUARTERLY
The new Middle East:
Shifting allies, enemies and loyalties

"Traditional principles and allegiances have given way to realpolitik." —Lina Khatib

The New Middle East examines the dramatic changes unfolding in the region as new rivalries, blocs and partnerships are formed – based not on ideology but on pragmatism.

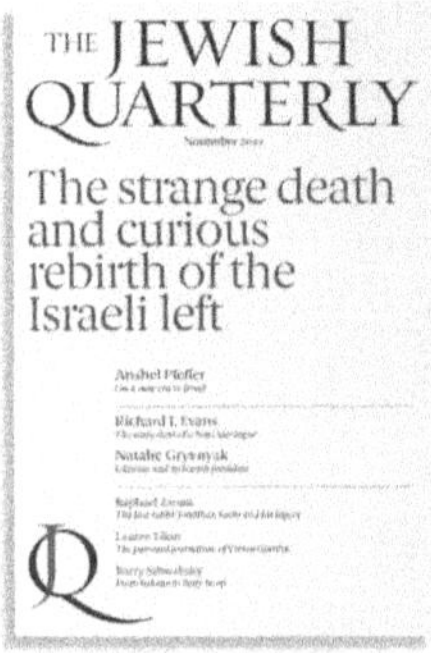
THE JEWISH QUARTERLY
The strange death and curious rebirth of the Israeli left

"The left has become the ideology that dare not speak its name." —Anshel Pfeffer

In *The Strange Death and Curious Rebirth of the Israeli Left,* Anshel Pfeffer takes the pulse of Israel's left wing, examining its health and prospects and dissecting the country's complex post-Netanyahu political reality.

"If ink on paper can reassemble a world ..."
—Rachel Kadish

The Jewish world of pre-war Europe was almost destroyed. If we hold up a lantern to that darkness, what can we discover about what was lost, what survived and what could have been?

"Younger writers were freed to think about specifically Jewish questions. [Their] work has a narrower appeal. Only time will tell if it is also a deeper one." —Adam Kirsch

After the Golden Age examines the current generation of leading American Jewish writers as they grapple with questions about religion, Israel, politics and multiculturalism.

"Iran's strategy is to eat away at American power, while legitimising its own role as a regional power with nuclear ambitions." —Kim Ghattas

Iran examines the motivations behind the country's changing role and influence in the Middle East, delving into the regime's secretive strategy and tactics.

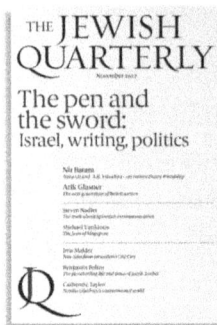

THE JEWISH QUARTERLY

The pen and the sword: Israel, writing, politics

Nir Baram
Arik Glasner
Jason Nadler
Michael Lindsaron
Jess Halder
Benjamin Belloc
Carlomena Taylor

"The process of saying goodbye to these two authors, who had been a visible presence in Israeli society for decades, is far from over."
—Nir Baram

The Pen and the Sword explores the efforts by successive generations of Israeli writers to grapple with their nation's difficult political questions.

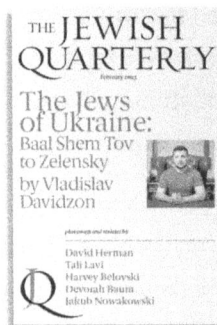

THE JEWISH QUARTERLY

The Jews of Ukraine: Baal Shem Tov to Zelensky by Vladislav Davidzon

David Herman
Tali Lavi
Harvey Belovski
Devorah Baum
Jakub Nowakowski

"Ukrainians voted for a mixture of Benny Hill and Boris Johnson, and they somehow wound up with Churchill."
—Vladislav Davidzon

The Jews of Ukraine explores the rich, tumultuous history of the Jews of Ukraine, who have played a pivotal role in modern Jewish life.

THE JEWISH QUARTERLY

THE AMIA BOMBING

JUSTICIA

An attack on Argentina's Jewish centre in 1994 killed 85 people. It remains unsolved. Why?

JAVIER SINAY

"I need to understand what no one yet understands: why, after nearly thirty years, there has been no justice." —Javier Sinay

The AMIA Bombing delves into the unresolved questions and political intrigue surrounding the terrorist attack that destroyed Buenos Aires' Jewish community centre in 1994.

THE JEWISH QUARTERLY — IVRIT

The language that makes a people

BEN JUDAH

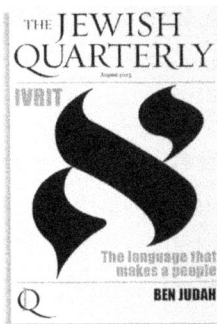

"Our religion, our story, is, at its heart, a love of this language and a refusal to let it go."
—Ben Judah

Ivrit explores the remarkable evolution and revival of Hebrew — a language whose trajectory charts the recent history of the Jewish people.

THE JEWISH QUARTERLY

DARK STAR

Elon Musk's Dangerous Turn   RICHARD COOKE

"Though he is already preparing to send astronauts to the moon, Musk has been consistently underestimated, and now the danger he presents is being underestimated as well."
—Richard Cooke

Dark Star explores the troubling political devolution of Elon Musk.

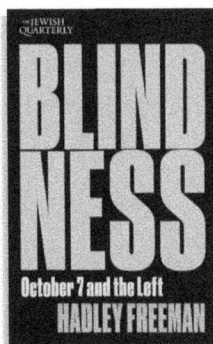

THE JEWISH QUARTERLY

BLINDNESS

October 7 and the Left
HADLEY FREEMAN

"October 7 was horrific. Then came October 8, and that's when Jews understood how hated they really are."
—Hadley Freeman

Blindness explores the willingness of progressives to abandon values they purport to represent.

WHITE WASH

Poland and the Jews
JAN GRABOWSKI

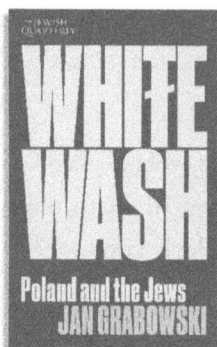

"Holocaust denial has now been replaced by a much more dangerous and insidious foe."
—Jan Grabowski

Whitewash examines how the Polish government, museums, schools and state institutions have been deployed to propagate a narrative of Polish national innocence during the Holocaust.

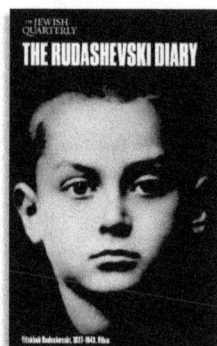

THE RUDASHEVSKI DIARY

Yitskhok Rudashevski, 1927–1943, Vilna

"Today I turned fifteen and live very much for tomorrow. I do not feel two ways about it. I see before me sun and sun and sun ..."

Yitskhok Rudashevski was transferred to the Vilna Ghetto when he was thirteen. His remarkable diary chronicles his hope, his despair and his experience of daily ghetto life.

MIND LESS

What happened to universities?
CARY NELSON

"Some programmes are well on their way to running Zionists out of their unit. That will put an end to complaints of antisemitism."
—Cary Nelson

Mindless shows how universities came to abandon a commitment to shared intellectual principles and slid towards conformity and indoctrination.

Add these past issues to your subscription when buying online.

Subscribe to The Jewish Quarterly and save.

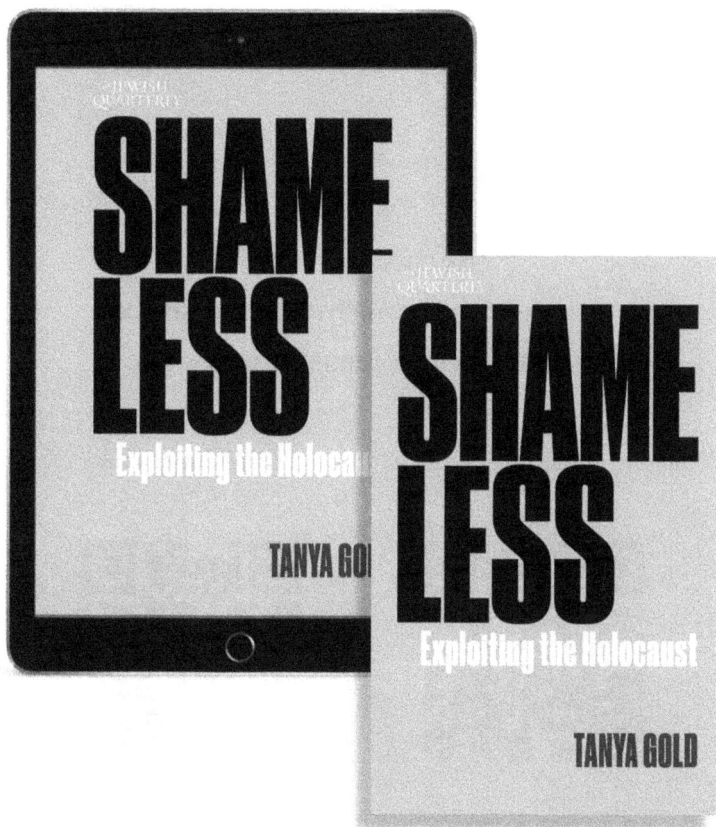

Enjoy free delivery of The Jewish Quarterly to your door, digital access to every issue of The Jewish Quarterly for one year, and exclusive special offers.

Forthcoming issue:

JQ261: Shameless: Exploiting the Holocaust

(August 2025)

Never miss an issue.
Subscribe and save.

- 1 year* print and digital subscription (4 issues) £42 GBP | $56 USD
- 1 year* digital subscription (4 issues) £25 GBP | $32 USD

Subscribe now:

Visit **jewishquarterly.com/subscribe**

Email **subscribe@jewishquarterly.com**

Scan one of these QR codes with your mobile device camera app:

Subscribe in £GBP   Subscribe in $USD

www.ingramcontent.com/pod-product-compliance
Lightning Source LLC
Chambersburg PA
CBHW021157090426
42740CB00008B/1128